Super Powers You Never Knew You Had

Develop Resilience
Build Confidence
Trust Yourself
Be Creative
Take Action
to
Achieve Your Goals

~ Lessons Learned from Positive Psychology ~

Dr. Carolynn Cobb

Almost Free Gift

As a thank you for purchasing this book, I am offering an Almost Free gift to you. It's a guided relaxation exercise that you can download in exchange for your contact information for my mailing list. I promise to keep your information confidential and be selective about mailing you. If you would like to be on the mailing list, https://superpowers.life/audio-file-sign-up/ to sign up.

I will send you a link to download the audio file.
Of course, you can unsubscribe from the mailing list at any time.

About the Author

Dr. Carolynn Cobb is a clinical psychologist in private practice in Texas. She currently specializes in clinical assessment, and personal growth and development.

Over her lifetime, Dr. Cobb has enjoyed several successful careers. In retail and call center management with multi-million-dollar revenues, Dr. Cobb gained insight into personalities, communications, project management, and leading teams. As a corporate trainer and consultant to Fortune 500 companies, Dr. Cobb taught skills in Quality Assurance, Motivation, Navigating Change, Leadership, and Management Development.

These skills, along with her down-to-earth unassuming personality, create the perfect combination and inspiration for insightful authorship.

Table of Contents

Who This Book is For

This book is for people who want to develop their ability to manage day-to-day problems with ease. The book is fun and entertaining, informative, and concise. By cutting out the psychobabble and hype, Dr. Cobb helps you look at life's challenges in a down-to-earth, realistic way. This book will help you develop the skills needed so you can solve your problems and achieve your goals.

What You Will Learn:

- How to bounce back from problems
- How to reduce stress
- How to listen to your inner voice
- How to increase your self-confidence
- How to be more creative
- How to make good decisions
- How to keep focused on the important things
- How to be hopeful
- How to trust yourself
- How to be more positive
- How to develop courage and conquer your fears
- How to stay motivated
- How to take action and get things done

Confessions of a Self-Help Junkie

Hi, my name is Carolynn and I'm a Self-Help Junkie.
Hi Carolynn!

As many people experience, I went through a period of floundering around wondering what the heck to do with my life. During my existential crisis, I began to devour self-help books. I read classic self-help such as Stephen R. Covey, Brian Tracy, Dr. Deepak Chopra, Dr. Wayne Dyer, Dr. Norman Vincent Peale, Emmet Fox, Viktor Frankl, and Napoleon Hill; and obscure authors no one had ever heard from before or since.

My bookshelves were full of motivational, new age, spiritual, psychology, and philosophy. But I never really found what I thought was THE ANSWER.

For me, the main concern at that time was to "find my purpose." I was certain that if I could just discover THE ANSWER ... I would make millions of dollars... find the right soul mate... be healthy... and happiness would prevail.

I attended workshops, made Miracle Wheels, and TRIED to meditate. Some authors seemed to speak directly to me at that time, and I felt some relief from the stress I was placing on myself to "be someone" or "do something." Other books were just not the right fit. Interestingly, later I might pick up the "wrong fit" book and it hit the spot. I think we are ready to learn certain things when we are ready.

In this book, I hope to "hit the spot" for you. If we are not a good fit today, maybe later the observations I am passing along will resonate and inspire you to transform your life!

Either way, I want to personally thank you for taking the time to purchase and read this book. It is a philosophy of life that has been developed through years of trial and error, struggles, observations, much study, and a little bit of WIGGLE.

Carolynn Cobb, PhD
Clinical Psychologist

Introduction

Life is full of changes. In 2015 to 2016 about 6.2 million workers changed from one occupation to another. [1] The marriage rate in the United States is 6.9 per 1000 population, while divorce rate is 3.2 per 1000.[2]

We all have a lot of stress in our lives. A study by the American Psychological Association indicates that most Americans suffer from **moderate to high stress** and are concerned mostly about money, work, the economy, family responsibilities, and health issues[3]. There are 40 million adults (18.1% of the population) living with an Anxiety Disorder in the US.[4] Worldwide 275 million people have an Anxiety disorder.[5]

Both Anxiety and Depression are global problems. More than 16.1 million American adults are affected by Major Depression and 268 million people worldwide. We are all affected by those numbers, whether directly, or by acquaintance.

Change and life stressors are part of the human experience. The way you deal with that change will dictate your success, your health, and your life experience. This

---

[1] Bureau of Labor Statistics, http://www.bls.gov/cps/

[2] Center for Disease Control and Prevention, Https://www.cdc.gov/nchs/fastats/marriage-divorce.htm

[3] American Psychological Association, Monitor on Psychology January 2011, Vol 42, No. 1, *Stressed in America.*

[4] *Mental Health Facts and Statistics.* NIMH Website. National Institute of Mental Health, Feb. 2013.

[5] Ritchie, H., & Roser, M., (2018). Mental Health. Published online at OurWorldinData.org. Retrieved from: https://ourworldindata.org/mental-health

book will help you manage life's challenges and end up on top.

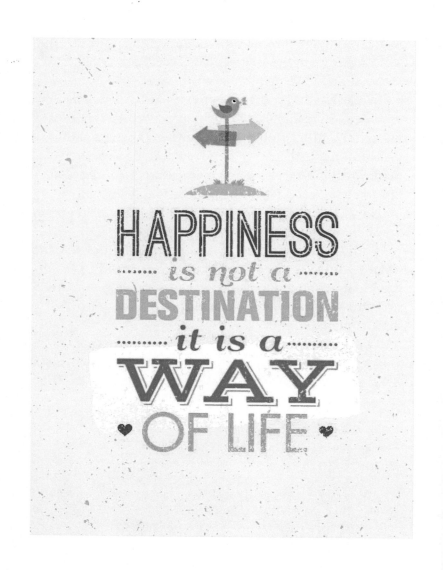

What is Wiggle?

Let me just get this off the table first, by wiggle, we are not talking about a worm, an exercise program, or a pole dancing technique.

The term WIGGLE or WIGGLING came about because of my SUPER POWER! Yes, I have a SUPER POWER.

Actually, I believe we all have Super Powers; some may need a little dusting off or polishing... but we all have them!

Super Powers are positive traits that when combined with each other create synergy resulting in something SUPER and POWERFUL. Super Powers are taking the positive traits we all have and developing them into strengths to use for good in our lives.

Positive Psychology, founded by Dr. Martin Seligman[6], refers to these traits as Characteristics and Virtues. Others

---

[6] Seligman, Martin. Pursuit of Happiness.org
http://www.pursuit-of-happiness.org/science-of-happiness/?gclid=CjwKCAjwtvnbBRA5EiwAcRvnphd7DGXyAIPxOwz_uJ
PKQ42OPOf1emxJ9YKFacPRJOLDyWbZz1ILpxoCwvUQAvD_BwE

call them strengths. In organizational psychology they are called competencies. One of mine is a habit of driving **intuitively**. When combined with other positive traits, my habit of driving and doing other things intuitively becomes what I call WIGGLING.

Intuitive driving is when traveling from point A to point B, if something comes up... such as a traffic jam, wreck, or roadblock... I just **WIGGLE** my way *around the problem* and **create a new path.**

This method of navigation often serves as a point of frustration for my friends, who do not trust my inner compass. I don't know why. Maybe it is because occasionally, I might go in circles around a loop in a small town. My friends do not miss the opportunity to point out, "Hey CC, I think we have passed by here before!"

We always arrive unharmed and no worse for the unorthodox route. Through the years, I have had good results with the wiggle method and continue to just *head out* without looking at a map.

So, what does this have to do with life and you?

After a few years of wiggling, I started to notice that I not only wiggle when driving, but I make unorthodox choices and take the "road less traveled" in many areas of my life. For instance, I earned a PhD through an on-line school, mostly while working a full-time job. There were of course face-to-face elements that required my presence, and practicums, internships, and post-doctoral fellowship to finally become licensed. However, it was an unorthodox approach.

Through the years I have learned how to find ways to overcome life's challenges in order to accomplish my goals. And I have been successful meeting those challenges.

Sometimes, the goal might have to be tweaked in order to move forward. At other times, you might have to go backwards so that you can progress toward your goal.

Through all the books, workshops, and EFFORT from the past, an *intuitive method of flowing through life* has emerged. I have developed the ability to face life with a combination of traits that create what I call the ability to WIGGLE.

These are TRAITS that we can DEVELOP. We do not have to be born with them but can LEARN them. Hey, somewhere along the way, I learned something!

Actually, I have learned quite a lot through the years about:

- How to live a **life of purpose**, with **passion**

- How to **transform yourself** into whatever you want to be, and

- When life throws you a roadblock, **take a different route** so you can move forward toward the destination of **your choosing.**

- **Create** the life you want to live.

This is what I want to share with you!
Wiggling can help you be a better:

- Worker
- Parent
- Teacher
- Student
- Partner
- Friend

When you allow yourself to let go of the preset, rigid, requirements that we all place on ourselves about:

- How to live
- What to do
- Which way to go

You are able to start **LISTENING** to your heart and **CREATE** the life you WANT!

You can **BLAST TROUGH** life problems and you will arrive at your **PURPOSE** without having to force things or struggle to make something happen.

"When I let go of what I am, I become what I might be."
Lao Tzu

Disclaimer

As a clinical psychologist, I come into contact with many people, and hear many life stories. The examples and cases in this book are compilations of individuals whom I have known. The names have been changed to protect the anonymity of the individuals.

How to Use Super Powers to Overcome Roadblocks

Face it, life does not go from point A to point B just the way we think it should.

Stuff happens! **Life happens**...

Researchers have found that the people who are able to be **RESILIENT** are able to overcome trauma, life stressors, change, adversity, and challenges much better.

In my definition, you are resilient when you are able to adapt to changes and overcome life's stressors with relative ease.

One of the difficulties when talking about resilience is the differing definitions of the idea. According to researchers[7] there have been over 100 definitions of

---

[7] Meredith, S., Sherbourne, C., Gaillot, S. J., Hansell, L., Ritschard, H. V., Parker, A. M., & Wrenn, G. (2011). *Promoting psychological resilience in the U.S.military*. SantaMonica, CA: RAND Corporation.

Resilience. Some common themes are:

- The requirement of a major traumatic event to occur

- Others believe resilience is making a positive change after the traumatic event occurs
- Another view is that resilience only requires that one adapts to the situation when going through major changes

With resilience, you are able to keep a positive attitude, regulate your emotions, be more optimistic, and see challenges as learning opportunities.

Wiggling is a form of resilience. In the example of driving, the roadblock is the obstacle to overcome. In life we encounter many obstacles and learning to deal with those effectively is a valued asset. Wiggling is one option that could help you navigate the everchanging terrain called life.

Of course, one of the most famous examples of overcoming challenges with an optimistic attitude is Thomas Edison, who saw each failure as simple information. He once said, "I have not failed. I've just found 10,000 ways that won't work."

Just think about that statement for a moment.

How many times have you given up something because it "didn't work out" or you felt like a "failure"? I propose that finding a different approach might have led to a better solution. Thomas Edison also said, *"Many of life's failures are people who did not realize how close they were to success when they gave up."*

Key Concept
If something is important to you...keep trying.

Don't give up at the first roadblock. Try a new path but stay on course. If you are headed North, maybe go North East or North West for a while, then turn back to North.

One thing to mention, is in the Key Concept above, it begins with "if something is important to you".

Do not waste your energy chasing butterflies if your goal is to grow daisies.

As the Cheshire Cat said to Alice's Adventures in Wonderland, *"How do you know which road to take if you don't know where you are going?"*

Charles Lutwidge Dodgson
Author by the pen name ~ Lewis Carroll

If you don't know what you want, that is fine. But realize you are not sure and approach the task as an **exploration**. There is nothing wrong with trying something out. Exploration gathers information as well, and with that information comes better decisions. Part of Wiggling is making informed decisions.

The Wiggle Method is a 7-step process for overcoming life's challenges by using your Super Powers. Following is the simple process used to WIGGLE.

The 7 Step Wiggle Process:

1. First take a deep breath and **BE CALM**. Don't panic. You've got this!

2. **LISTEN** to your heart. Follow your intuition.

3. Use the **KNOWLEDGE** you already have, and **COMMON SENSE.**

4. Evaluate the **ALTERNATIVES**.

5. Use **CREATIVITY** to think of any additional alternatives.

6. Make an educated **DECISION.**

7. **TAKE ACTION!**

At each step of the WIGGLE process, you will find certain Super Powers to be very useful. They help you prepare for the step and they help you work through the issue with which you are currently dealing.

Next, we will take a look at each of these steps, which Super Powers are used during that phase, and learn how to develop those Super Powers.

Step 1: Stay Calm

Using Self-Confidence, Spirituality, Inner Peace, and Optimism

The first step to overcoming roadblocks is stay calm or *don't freak out*. How do you stay calm when the world is falling apart around you?

It helps to have some Super Power strengths. In this case, those are things like self-confidence, spirituality, inner peace, and optimism.

I know that I can usually get anywhere by wiggling. I am **confident** in the process. Most people think that is the craziest way to get about and they have no hope that it will work. And those are the people who would get dreadfully lost because they do not have the foundation to wiggle. The foundation of certain traits or strengths that come together as my wiggle.

Why do I know it will work? Because I have the experience that it does work.
How did I get that experience? By trial and error.

I used the **power of curiosity** to explore new places and see what happens. By using the **power of observation,** I made a mental note that it can work. I learned not to turn into the ocean or drive into the lake.

By the way, the only place I have ever had a hard time navigating without a map is Salt Lake City, Utah. If you are not familiar with Salt Lake City, everything is setup to be measured or described from point zero, which is the Mormon Tabernacle. It is like a bullseye target with the church in the middle. Totally confused me! When traveling there, I had to actually buy a map in the days before apps.

Staying Calm = Reducing Stress

Staying calm is another way to say, don't stress out. It is hard to stay calm when you are in the middle of a crisis. The best defense with stress is a good offense. That is, prepare yourself by learning to hold back anxiety when you start to feel it rise.

Stress is a response to a threat or situation. It is the way your body lets you know there is an urgent problem that needs your attention. In nature, the types of threats are things like an attacking tiger. Animals know they'd better run or get eaten! That is called "fight or flight."

In our society the threat might be something like an 18-wheeler barreling down on you. That kicks in your body's "fight or flight" response. You might be stressed out over many things in the day. Your child comes home and says, "I need these things for school tomorrow." That can cause all kinds of stress. You have to now drop everything and run out to find this laundry list and you have to pay extra money you were not planning on spending. At work you may get a stressful call, or your boss expects you to do something that puts pressure on you.

Every day you are bombarded with stressful situations. Each event adds a bit of stress to your day. If you put off that stress response repeatedly anxiety begins to develop.

Anxiety builds up in your body and begins to affect your health. It may cause headaches, high blood pressure, sweaty palms, upset stomach, or rapid heartbeat. Some people may think they are having a heart attack but find out it is a panic attack. You want to reduce stress in your life before it becomes a health concern.

In general, there are many ways to develop the ability to stay calm or reduce your level of stress about a situation. You could practice meditation, yoga, progressive relaxation, visualization, biofeedback, breathing techniques, mindfulness, aroma therapy, exercise, run, lift weights, drink less caffeine, or take up a hobby that brings you joy. Each of these topics could be a book in itself.

The point is, there are many avenues you can take to learn to stay calm, quiet the chatter and anxiety in your mind and body. Do not forget that the mind and body are connected and by improving one aspect you will most likely see benefits in other areas.

Warning: I am going to suggest many things in this book. Do not do them all at once; for one thing, you will have no clue what works for you and what does not. Secondly, it would be way too many things to add to your routine. Read through the book and make note of what you might like to try. Then think it over and do one or two of them for a month. See how it suits you.

There are exercises in the Appendix to give some of these ideas a try. I also have a companion workbook available to help keep track of activities and add structure to your chosen changes. Check it out if you would like a printed set of exercises and activities. Go to https://superpowers.life/wiggle-workbook-sign-up/ for the workbook download.

Reduce Stress by Your Actions

One thing that causes a lot of stress is being late all the time. When in college, just after high school, I used to be the *sleep in, hit snooze 3-times, throw on some sweats, and race off to class type.* I was always late, causing the disdain of professors. I would park in the "wrong" places and get campus parking tickets, causing financial stress. I even tried *doing math* in the morning. That is, setting the clock forward 1 hour or 45 minutes to "fool" myself. *Well, it's really 7:15 or is it 6:00, I don't know...snooze...*

It was not pretty.

Learn to be on-time

Somewhere along the way I finally started being the *early person.* I'm the one at the airport hours before my flight. When traffic jams happen on the way somewhere, I am cool because I have given myself plenty of time to get there. It is such a relief to be on-time.

Avoid Conflict

Another way to reduce stress by your actions is to avoid useless conflict. There are some people who just seem to want to get into a fight with others. They bump into you at the store and it is your fault. They steal the parking space when you have your blinker flashing. They cut in line. They give you "honest feedback" just so they can hear themselves talk or take the wind out of your sails.

The key is don't take the bait.

These people are baiting you to fight with them. They are angry and irritable. Do not let their bad mood become your day. I am not saying back down when something is important to you. I am saying, "Choose Your Battles". Stop and think one second. Is this worth your blood pressure rising? Is it worth your stress level building? As you get better at holding your tongue and avoiding the people who are trying to push your buttons, you will find your life is much calmer.

Exercise

Another way to reduce stress by your actions is to add more exercise to your daily routine. Don't just do it once and call it a day. Increase your exercise for at least a month at regular intervals (10 minutes, 20 minutes, 30 minutes etc.) throughout the week. Build your stamina as you are able. This will help you be calm, sleep better, and improve your breathing, which is important to calming your body and your mind.

Use Cool Gadgets

These days there are many apps and gadgets to help you reduce stress and be healthy. You can monitor your breathing, sleep, and heart rate. You can track your steps and your food intake. You can set alarms to remind yourself to do important tasks, so you won't have to worry about it. Check out the app store of your choosing and see what goodies you can find.

Meditation, Yoga, Relaxation

There seems to be a lot of focus on Mindfulness Meditation these days. My simplified definition of being mindful is being aware and able to control the direction of your thoughts. To do this you will need to develop the ability to observe your thoughts, which is discussed later in this book. After recognizing your thoughts, you will then learn to control them.

I am not talking about someone else controlling what you think, this is you realizing, "Oh, I am beating myself up mentally." That is being mindful of your thought. Then you might think, "That is not what I want to do, I want to think about the ways I will be successful." The next step is to focus your attention on the new thought. You might visualize yourself being successful at whatever it is you want to do.

Yoga

Yoga is a favorite of many people for reducing stress and creating sound bodies. Yoga helps you learn to breathe correctly, which also reduces the levels of stress in your body and helps clear your mind. Yoga helps you learn to focus and to be patient with yourself, which then transfers to patience with other people.

Relaxation Techniques

The *freebee* I offer at the beginning of this book is a guided relaxation designed to help you reduce stress. There are many of these imagery and relaxation meditations available from many sources. It is often good to create your own relaxation audio so that the imagery can be customized to your motivating triggers and to your goals. You can have special music that helps you relax. Try out the relaxation audio I have available for free and then make one of your own.

To increase your level of calm, or reduce your stress level, choose one of these methods and spend at least a month practicing the technique. You don't have to be an expert to test something out and decide if it is what you want to pursue. Try it for at least 1 month to get the feel for it and decide if it is something you want to continue.

Check the Appendix for Stress Reduction Exercises

Developing Self-Confidence

The first Super Power of Being Calm is Self-Confidence. Just as I am confident with my WIGGLE, you can develop confidence with the way you WIGGLE. The way you develop that confidence is by proving to yourself that you can do it.

The **key** to building confidence is taking small steps and trying it out. **Then notice when you are successful.**

The hardest thing for many people is to realize that they had a success, because they want it to be perfect and complete. We will talk more about taking small steps and achieving measurable success later. But for now, the key to remember is you build **Self-Confidence** by observing yourself doing well.

"People are like stained-glass windows. They sparkle and shine when the sun is out, but when the darkness sets in their true beauty is revealed only if there is light from within."

Elisabeth Kubler-Ross
Psychiatrist and Author On Death and Dying

There is a self-confidence starter exercise in the Appendix.

Developing Inner Peace

It can be very difficult to have inner peace when you have a lot of anxiety and stress in your life. One tool that many are finding helpful is adult coloring books. As you focus on the detail of coloring, your mind can begin to quiet some. If you are particularly angry, you could use all red color to express that anger. Or if you are feeling rebellious, you could draw outside the lines. Mostly joking here. But coloring does bring calm to many people. When you are done there is a sense of accomplishment as well.

Other hobbies such as making model cars, boats, or planes can have the same type of effect. As you focus on the details of the task at hand, you forget some of those pesky things that are causing the stress.

Playing an instrument or listening to music can provide peace. Walking in nature is another helpful activity. As you walk you are required to breathe better and deeper. You can enjoy the sights and sounds of nature that are calming to most people.

Spirituality

One way we feel a sense of peace and calm is through spirituality. Some people are religious in one way or another. I am talking about having a connection with nature, and universal spirit. You may think of this as a deity. It does not matter what religion you apply, having a connection with nature will bring about a sense of calm and peace.

Go out in nature and be. Just spend time there. Breathe clean air, watch the water flow, listen to the birds and coyotes. Take some time to enjoy nature. Think about how incredible nature is...connect with spirit. By the way this is also mindfulness as you are slowing your thoughts and focusing on the elements of nature, you are mindful.

If you live in a large city, go to a park and enjoy the nature available. Watch the children play on the playscapes. Enjoy the laughter they project as they carelessly go about their day. There is a wonderous spirit in the laughter of children.

"To me there is no picture so beautiful as smiling, bright-eyed, happy children; no music so sweet as their clear and ringing laughter."

P.T. Barnum
Founder Barnum & Baily Circus

Optimism

Having optimism in the face of negative thoughts is a hard one. To me, the key is to see the other side of the coin… Not to be Pollyanna Happy. Some people chose to see what they call the realistic side of things and try to think of all the bad things that can happen. I call that worrying.

Worry has its benefits. It allows us to prepare ourselves for possible unfortunate occurrences. However, when we allow the worry to consume our lives and cause illness in our body, it is too much.

If you are one who relies on worry possibly too much, you might try gently pushing the negative thoughts aside when you notice them.

First you have to use metacognition to think about your thinking. That is, start paying attention to what you are thinking. When you realize that you are having negative thoughts, just push them aside and replace them with an alternative thought. Substitute one that is kind of neutral.

It may be fairly difficult to realize what you are thinking. So, try this little exercise for a while to catch your thoughts. Then push them aside after you can recognize them.

Thought Catching Exercise

1. Sit alone in a room, in a comfortable chair

2. Set an alarm on your phone for 1 min

3. When the alarm goes off – immediately write down what you were thinking at that moment.

4. Do it again and again for at least 5 times

5. Then try mentally watching your thoughts as if they were butterflies' dancing in the sky.

If that is too much metaphor, just think about your thoughts without the timer.

Catch them on your own without having a timer to stop you. Write down what you are thinking.

Look at your list, are most of the thoughts positive? Or negative? Are they optimistic or pessimistic?

Once you are able to realize what you are thinking. Try shoving a thought aside. Just say "not now" to it and think of something else. As you practice this, you will become better at it and able to move some of your thinking to a more neutral state, rather than allowing so much negativity in your thought processes.

That is the first step: Stay calm in the face of the challenge. It helps to use the Super Powers of Self

Confidence, Spirituality, Inner Peace, and Optimism to help maintain a sense of calm when you are faced with life's challenges.

You don't have to use them all. By developing these Super Powers you will equip yourself with the ability to deal with problems.

Now let's look at ways to develop the Super Powers of step two.

Step 2: Listen to Your Heart

Using Intuition, Hope, and Faith

" Have the Courage to Follow Your Heart and Intuition. They somehow already know what you truly want to become. Everything else is secondary. "

Steve Jobs
Chairman, CEO, and co-founder Apple, Inc.

Step two involves listening to your heart so you know what to do. This step uses **Intuition, Hope,** and **Faith** which are also elements of the Super Powers **Courage** and **Trust**. Some of the methods that help develop **Calm** will also help develop these Super Powers.

In order to know your heart's desires, you have to start with **listening.** The best listening happens in quiet times. Find a place that is quiet. Your place could be a room, or a place in nature, such as a park. Go to this quiet place and sit. Just sit quietly. Close your eyes and try to quiet your mind.

I realize that is almost impossible for some people. I used to be one of you. I really learned to quiet my mind when I traveled for work all the time. I was forced to sit in airports, on planes, driving etcetera. When you are forced to sit for many hours, you get tired of watching movies on your devices. You grow weary from emails and talking on the phone or looking at social media. Finally, you learn to sit and quiet your mind. To just be.

"To make the right choices in life, you have to get in touch with your soul. To do this, you need to experience solitude, which most people are afraid of, because in the silence you hear the truth and know the solutions."

Deepak Chopra
Author, Public Speaker, Alternative Medicine Advocate

After your mind is still, as if it were a calm pond with no waves on the water, pick up a thought and toss it in the still water. Watch the ripples echo out from the core. Allow those thoughts to pass.

Then be still again. From this slowing of the thoughts you should be able to listen to your heart. You can learn what your heart is telling you to do. Then you can begin to make small steps toward your heart's desire.

As we discussed earlier, if you have some small successes you will find that you begin to trust yourself and you have hope that by planting seeds, they will bear fruit. It's just like children learning to walk, they learn to crawl first... then sit up... stand... and finally take those first steps.

What I am saying is that you need to make some attempts that are small. Don't try to "leap tall buildings in a single bound" at first.

Note: This is slightly different from thought catching I discussed earlier. With this, you are trying to LISTEN to your inner voice to gain CLARITY.

You can get in a quiet state and then ask a simple question, such as:

- What should I do next?

- Who is the right candidate for the job?

- Should I add that extra volunteer position to my workload?

- How will this help me move forward?

- Will it help me move forward?

Then, wait for the answer. The answer may not be the voice of James Earl Jones booming down on you. It may be an image of something that will tell you the answer. It may be something familiar to you such as a deceased pet, or family member. Or it might be something new to you.

Once I was meditating and the image of a dragonfly came to me. I used to have an Irish Setter named Peeper, who loved to chase dragonflies. So that dragonfly symbolized my dog in my interpretation. He was a sweet dog and used to talk all the time. He was very chatty.

In this particular meditation, I was thinking about what I should do about a situation at work. One thought I had was to discuss the problem with a coworker, but I was not sure who I could trust with the situation. I could not figure out why the image of the dragonfly came to me. Then finally, I realized that there was a manager in another department with the last name of Peabody. My mind was telling me to talk to Peabody by sending me the symbol of the dog Peeper. Only my mind would come up with that symbol to tell me, "Go talk to Peabody."

If you think about the imagery you receive, you will realize what your heart and brain are trying to tell you. Such was the case of Charles.

The Case of Charles

Charles is a 41-year-old, who was going through a career crisis. He was frustrated, and tired of working hard at a job that no longer brought him joy. He felt stuck because he needed to make a certain amount of money, and his job as a warehouse foreman was the only thing he knew how to do. After several discussions and looking inward with the techniques we have discussed above, Charles decided he really wanted to get out of the warehouse and into nature. If he could just figure out how to make a living in nature, he would be happy. However, he had no hope that he could ever work in nature. He felt it was an unrealistic dream.

Think about his situation a moment. What would you suggest to your friend Charles if he approached you with this problem?

Some would agree with him that his dream is unrealistic, and he needs to remain at the warehouse job to support his family.

Others might tell him to forget his responsibilities and do what he wants to do...no matter what.

Charles actually did find a way to support his family and become involved in nature. He began by volunteering in a program in which he and other volunteers planted trees in a local forest to regenerate the area. He then took a landscaping class.

Doing these things helped him feel better and he started finding more ways to become involved in nature. He finally ended up starting his own landscaping business on the weekends. Eventually, that business became a full-time endeavor and he was able to leave the warehouse job.

It took a lot of courage and trust for Charles to make the leap to begin his business and to finally work full-time in landscaping. He did not leap off a cliff wildly but instead, he used **common sense** to take those small steps to reach his goal. We will talk more about common sense later as it is an important Super Power.

Intuition

As I mentioned earlier, when I wiggle, I drive intuitively. That is, I use an inner compass to guide me. Even if there are mountains and curvy roads, trees, or skyscrapers, I can find my way to my destination. If you can develop an inner compass for your life, you will be able to listen to your heart and know what is right for you.

There is no need to worry about what is your purpose, because you know what is right to do. You begin to just know. There is no worry about finding your passion because you already know in your heart what it is...you have intuition to guide your life.

Sometimes you may not know how you are going to accomplish the goal, but you know what it is and where you want to end. Sometimes it is not as much about knowing what is right, as it is a feeling that something is wrong for you. For instance, you may get a feeling that you are in the wrong job, or dating the wrong person, or doing things in your life that do not feel comfortable to you. With an inner compass you can feel it when things are amiss.

Great, so how do you get intuition? **Through listening.** You have to stop talking, **stop worrying**, and stop the chatter. The chatter causes self-doubt and uncertainty. When you are able to listen to your soul, you are able to **know.**

Sometimes when we are busy trying to make things happen we push too hard. We try to force things by setting deadlines and trying to commit ourselves to things. We try to be "All In" or not do the thing at all.

Life is full of variety. It is like a sliding scale rather than a set number of increments. I am not saying that effort is bad, but it has its place. Sometimes it is better to stop and quiet your mind.

Winston Churchill reportedly used to sleep on decisions before making them. If you are feeling pressured about something, you probably are not in the right frame of mind to make a decision. So, give yourself a break and put that decision off for a brief period, then you can revisit it and make the decision with a clear head. Listen to your heart and you will know what is right for you. Allow yourself to dream.

Hope

Hope is the expectation of something good in your life. Without hope we have little reason to look forward to tomorrow. Those who lack hope are usually depressed or going through a period of emotional drought.

One of the best examples of Hope to me is a place called Community First Village in Austin, TX. Community First is a sustainable housing project created by Mobile Loaves & Fishes[8]. They have created a community of tiny homes that are housing for those who were once homeless. There are other amenities in the community as well, such as a medical facility, a community garden in

---

[8] Mobile Loaves & Fishes https://mlf.org

which they grow food that the residents eat, and an outdoor theater. The residents are able to reestablish their lives and gain Hope for their future.

To me this is the epitome of Hope. When you have the expectation that something good can come into your life, that tomorrow will be worth living, you have Hope.

Without Hope we become listless, have little motivation, are apathetic, and depressed. The worse we feel the worse it gets. So, the question is...How to develop Hope if you have none?

First, let me say that if you are in a deep despair, seek professional help. You may not be able to pull out of this without some assistance. Having said that, there are some simple things that we can do to lift our spirits and provide some hope.

1. Exercise, preferably in nature. By getting out in nature in the sunlight we are activating our brains and our bodies. Sunlight enhances our mood. It increases levels of serotonin in the brain and can help reduce feelings of stress. Sunlight also helps your brain produce melatonin, which in turn helps you sleep better.

2. Even if you do not want to, engage with others. Be social in some way. If you live alone, go out of your house and attend some event where there will be other people. Talk to some people if you can. If you have friends, give them a call or text with them. Go to your local church or

find a support group. Attend a lecture.

3. Volunteer to help others. It is an interesting phenomenon, when we help others we give ourselves the gift of Hope. There is reportedly a release of serotonin when we act with kindness toward others. Volunteering on a regular basis helps develop a sense of Hope.

"It is one of the beautiful compensations in this life that no one can sincerely try to help another without helping himself."

Ralph Waldo Emerson
Writer, Philosopher, and Poet

One way to do something for others is by making a *Random Act of Kindness.* This is really a simple task, you just do something nice for someone. I can't even count the times I have been in the Starbucks line and the barista said, "The car in front of you paid for your coffee!" I of course, then paid it forward for the car behind me. This has actually happened so many times, I think Starbucks does it themselves. Anyway, it is a bright moment in my day. Do something random for someone you don't know.

You can probably think of a dozen things you could do for other people fairly easily.

- Buy someone a coffee

- Buy a lottery ticket and give it to a stranger

- Let someone in line in front of you at the store

- Hold the door open for someone

- Give a flower to a stranger

- Let that other car park in the space you were coveting.

Faith

Faith is believing and letting go. It is trust. Trust in yourself, in that spiritual element, and in other people. Oh dear, that's a hard one. Yep, sometimes we have to be vulnerable and have faith in others. We can't do everything on our own. We have to learn how to delegate some things and allow other people the respect to have faith that they can accomplish the task. This is true in our personal lives as well as in business.

Some of the best managers I have ever worked with are the ones who know how to delegate. They provide the training, the knowledge, the resources and once a person is ready and can handle the load, they delegate without hovering. They let the person do the job. Every now and then they check back and see if more support is needed, but the person has the reins.

We have to be able to have that kind of faith in ourselves. As you can readily see these Super Powers build on each other. Intuition and hope help you have faith. These Super Powers help you build the self-confidence that you can do the thing you want to do.

The good thing is that as we develop one strength, we are helping bolster the other traits. So, effort in one area helps you meet the challenges in your life in general. You are building mental and psychological fitness.

Develop Courage

Courage is usually developed by some method of exposure, and inoculation.

One first step could be to write down your specific fears. For instance, if you are afraid of looking like a fool in public or being the center of attention. You can write down what it is and memories you might have of the first time you started feeling this way.

By looking back at those incidences that created the initial feeling, you are starting to face the fear. The first step to overcoming the fear is to understand it and recognize that it is holding you back.

Look at Past Actions

One of the best ways to foretell the future is to look at the past. Think about and write down how you have been courageous in the past. Maybe you have not been successful at facing this particular fear, but you have been able to do other things with the courage and strength you are seeking.

Sometimes this is a difficult task, because when we are feeling as if we have no courage, it is hard to see the times when we have exemplified courage. This is when talking to a professional might be helpful. They can see things from a different perspective and help you see them.

Look for Role Models

You might observe others who you consider to be courageous.

What do they do?

Why is it courageous?

Is there a way you can emulate their behavior?

If you are able to recognize times when you have been courageous, think about how you can apply that feeling to this situation.

It might help to think through, and write down, some of the possible scenarios that might come up. If you are afraid of looking like a fool in public, think about what you can do when you start feeling that way.

Sometimes we feel more confident when we wear certain clothing or get a haircut. So, one way you could plan your scenario would be to get up and dress the way that makes you feel most confident. Then practice in your head, driving to the location and visualize getting out of the car. At that point, that might be enough. Stop and realize that was a success to get that far. Then take a break.

The next time you push yourself a little further. One trick is to push yourself, **without overdoing it**. Take your time and take small steps. Again, it might be best to seek help from a professional. Guided meditation might help you be able to face your fears.

Usually taking small steps is a good way to go. I have a friend who used to have a fear of talking to people. In order to push himself in a small way, he decided to try talking to people when in an elevator. Since he was only in the elevator for a short period, it couldn't go too wrong.

So, whenever he was riding an elevator with one other person, he would say something nice about the person, like compliment their shoes or tie. The conversation didn't last long, and he was able to get over his fear of talking to strangers by taking small steps.

Affirmations

You might find that affirmations can help you bolster your courage. Create affirmations that you can believe. Repeat them until you do believe them. Make them second nature. Then when the time arrives to face the fear, gently bring that affirmation into your mind. It will provide comfort and help bolster your courage.

Typically, affirmations are short statements that start with "I am..." Affirmations are stated in present tense even if the thing has not happened in your current reality.

It helps to use words that stimulate an emotional response and use action words. Affirmations are personal in nature and have less impact if you try to use canned statements that someone else created.

Having said that, here are some sample affirmations, just for examples:

- I am brave and eloquent as I accept my award for top salesperson.

- I am excited and joyful as I climb to the top of Mt. Rainier.

- I am at peace as I play my guitar.

- I am brilliant and proud as I graduate with honors.

- I am thrilled to see my book as a Best Seller.

There is an affirmation writing exercise in the Appendix.

Trust Yourself

In this case, we are talking about self-trust. The belief that you can accomplish your goals. As with Courage, you can show yourself that you are trustworthy by taking small steps and meeting your expectations to accomplish your goals. As you have success, you will begin to listen to your inner voice more and trust that it knows what the heck it is talking about.

Now, do NOT listen to that nagging voice that tells you things are not going to work out the way you want. It is WRONG. There will be hurdles to jump along the way. Even Dorothy had problems to face along the "yellow brick road." In fact, that was the whole premise. She had to face her fears in order to get home right?

We all have the ability to listen to our inner voice and do what is right for us. However, all the extra noise and hubbub that our minds create from worry, anxiety, stress keep us from hearing our true selves. Trusting in one's self combines the following abilities:

- To be calm

- To listen to your heart

- To be courageous and brave

- To follow the guidance offered by your inner voice

- To take actions with the belief (or faith) that it will work

That is a lot to ask when you are not used to doing it. So, be kind to yourself and set reasonable expectations.

Don't expect to run a marathon before you begin to walk around the block.

Step 3: Use the Knowledge You Already Have, and Common Sense

Use Your Thinking Skills, Good Judgment, and Common Sense

Charles in the example above used the knowledge he built through taking classes and studying landscaping, along with common sense to know when and how to start his own business. When overcoming roadblocks in life, we have to take a moment to realize what we know and how it will help us. In driving, we may know that the interstate ahead is under construction or there is a fire ahead. With that knowledge we can use the common sense to make a judgment call.

Hint: Don't go toward the fire!

There are methods you can use to practice critical thinking and analysis. One thing you can do to build critical thinking skills is to begin playing strategy games, such as chess.

Why? Because in chess you have to think several moves ahead all the time. If you only move one step at a time, you will lose. You have to look at not only your possible moves, but the "what if" scenarios of the other player. *If I do X, she might do Y...*

By playing such games, you will develop the ability to analyze your possible choices.

Examine both sides of the coin:

Another method to use when developing critical thinking skills is to look at the situation from the "other" point of view. There is always more than one side of an argument or a situation. For just a brief moment, take your feelings out of your mind and look at it from the other side of the coin. **Be objective.** Many things are polar in perspective.

Light / Dark
Up / Down
Hot / Cold
Rich / Poor

Let's say you have always loved country music. You have never even considered listening to any other type of music. As an exercise to expand your ability to think about country music, you could spend some time with other types of music. Try them out. Listen to Rap. Think about how it is different and yet the same as country music. Listen to Jazz. *Think about how great it is...* oops, those personal preferences just slide right in there.

Anyway, you get the point. To broaden your ability to think about things, look at it from a different perspective.

Critical Thinking **REQUIRES Thinking**

The key point here is that sometimes we just amble through life without thinking. We do the same things all the time. We defer to others to make decisions for us.

In order to be an active participant in your own life, you have to put on the "big kid pants" and start making some decisions for yourself.

As a psychologist I of course have paperwork for people to fill out when they come in the door. The typical stuff right. There is the page with the name and address information, the history information, and the page we call the informed consent. What that means is that you understand the rules of the game... what are the limitations of confidentiality etc. Do you read those?

So many people come in and just sign without reading. I could write on that page that they are giving me their house, car, or any other prized possession and they would sign away, without reading it. They are just going through the motions without thinking. Don't sign your life away without reading the fine print.

Common Sense

It is strange to me to even write about common sense. The name defines itself. But, many people are so busy trying to be something they are not. Or they are too stressed out to stop a moment and think, hey, does this make sense? Is this what any prudent person would call good judgment?

- Don't do things because you think someone else wants you to do it

- Don't do things that are outrageously risky

- Think through the consequences before acting

Take Care of Business

Part of common sense is to first take care of the things that need handling, for instance, making a living. If you are trying to "find" your true calling or your "purpose" in life, you will not find it if you are desperate and unemployed.

There are several psychological theories about what motivates people, one of them is Maslow's theory in which he proposed there is a hierarchy of needs that people have to go through to reach the highest level of "Self-actualization". The bottom level that everyone needs includes the fundamentals, the basic food, water, sleep etc.

That is what I mean by take care of business first. If you do not have a job, get one. It does not have to be the greatest job in the world. It is to provide you with the fundamentals. I have had several jobs I called "job jobs," not career makers. It is just common sense to do what you have to so that you can then move forward.

By the way, sometimes those "job jobs" can turn into true opportunities. So, don't be a slacker when you are there. Give it good effort and you might be surprised what transpires.

Interesting tidbit. *Common Sense* is the name of a booklet produced by Thomas Paine in 1776 to persuade the colonists to fight for independence. This document is thought to have ignited the American Revolution. It is still sold. Common Sense has always been a great Super Power.

"Common sense is the knack of seeing things as they are, and doing things as they ought to be done."

Henry Wheeler Shaw
American humorist, who wrote under the pen name
Josh Billings

Step 3 allows us to be smart with our Wiggling. Think about what we know, use that knowledge wisely, and "do things as they ought to be done" with common sense.

In the next chapter we build on this knowledge, so we can later make excellent decisions.

Step 4: Evaluate the Alternatives

Using Analysis and Observation

"To observe attentively is to remember distinctly"

Edgar Allen Poe
American writer, editor, and literary critic

Step 4 builds on the knowledge and common-sense judgment of Step 3. When presented with several options or choices we have to use the **power of analysis** to determine which is the right one.

Analysis

One way to review the alternatives is the old tried and true Pro / Con list. Simply make a list of all the reasons in favor of alternative X and all the reasons it stinks.

Do that for each choice. In the end, the answer will be apparent.

One possible problem will come up if you have not set aside your preconceived notions and personal preferences. You have to start with a clean slate so that the options have a chance. Be objective.

Because I prefer cheese cake, I will probably always find a way that cheese cake is the "best" choice for a desert I am bringing to a function. Is it really? Who knows? But I am biased and will most likely come to that conclusion. There is an error in my thinking regarding cheese cake.

Be sure you do not have biases that cause errors in your thinking.

Don't forget to apply all the knowledge you already have to your analysis.

Sample analysis:

In our driving scenario we see a roadblock up ahead.
- Choice A: wait in the long backup
- Choice B: turn right, go for a while, then turn back to the direction you were going
- Choice C: turn left, go for a while, then turn back to the direction you were going

If we think about what we already know in this situation it makes the decision easy. Why?

Because we know that to the **right is a football stadium** and this is **Saturday** and the local college team is playing. So, now we know what to do. Simple scenario, but you get the point, right?
Think it through...

1. What do you know?

2. How does that contribute to your decision?

3. Is there an alternative I did not mention?
    YES

4. What is it?

Well, you could go backwards for a while, then take a new route. It is possible that taking a step backwards is sometimes the best choice.

You could also park your car and get on a train to reach your destination. **Be creative.**

Next, we will explore more about being creative.

Step 5: Use Creativity to Think of Any Additional Alternatives

Using Creativity, Flexibility, and Curiosity

"Whatever the mind of man can conceive and believe, it can achieve."

Napoleon Hill
Author, Think and Grow Rich

Step 5 in our Wiggle method is to use creativity to find new alternatives. For people who think they are not creative, it is really hard to try to be creative. As you push yourself to explore your creativity you will be able to find new and inventive ways to accomplish your goals.

BE CREATIVE

There are many ways to become more creative. Take an art class. Go to a craft store and buy some kind of kit to make something.

In a former career, I was a consultant in the Call Center industry, which allowed me to travel all over the US and to many foreign countries. The best part for me was looking at different shops, museums, and art galleries. One day in Seattle, I fell in love with the most beautiful thing I had ever seen... Blown Glass. I actually became tearful when I saw this piece and I thought to myself, if I could only make something like that my life would be complete.

I had never made anything with glass and had no clue what it took to become a glass blower. But my heart ached for it. So, I started looking for opportunities to learn something about glass. I used my curiosity about things to learn as much as I could from the internet or from gallery owners.

Then I found a class at a gallery on the weekends. My first class was making glass beads. The second class was making paper weights. Finally, I found some guys at an art fair who said they needed people to help out in the studio. They later told me people ask all the time about learning to blow glass, but they never show up to actually work for free as an assistant.

Well, I did. I would travel all week, then spend the weekend in the glass shop, standing in front of a 2400 degree furnace all day on concrete floors. Not a glamorous endeavor. Every now and then I would actually get to make something. My first "piece" was a glob of clear glass with somewhat of a cup shape. It is awful, but I still have it.

After years of doing this, taking classes, and visiting glass shops and galleries all over the world, I finally learned enough to actually make some decent pieces. The moral of the story is that Creativity is sometimes very hard work. It is not always glamorous, or cute. But it does bring great satisfaction. Developing your creative side will allow you to come up with ideas that help you navigate through life.

What would you like to do to be more creative?

How can you start doing that activity in the near future?

Even if you are unable to afford taking a class or buy art materials at this time, you can find ways to be more creative. Think about trying something new with cooking. You could try new spices or cook something you have never made before. Be creative with the presentation of your food.

Try writing a poem or a song.

With a little effort, you can be more creative than you are today. It also helps to have a burning desire or passion for something.

"Passion is one great force that unleashes creativity, because if you're passionate about something, then you're more willing to take risks.

Yo-Yo Ma
French-born American cellist

I personally dislike all the hype about *"finding your passion."* If it is your passion it is not lost and has no need to be "found." The problem is that everyone wants to know and label their great passion. As mentioned above, by **listening** you will **know** your passion. You will not have to look for or label it.

Flexibility

Flexibility is bending without breaking. We want to be flexible because rigidity does not lead to additional options. Would you like to eat at a restaurant that only serves one thing? No options? You certainly don't want to be stuck with no options in life.

Don't keep doing the same thing over and over and expecting something to be different. Life does not change unless we do.

We all have routines. The alarm goes off and we get up. What do you do first? What next?

To develop a little flexibility, try mixing up the order a little. I'm not saying wear your clothes inside out or anything too risky.

Just try being more flexible. "Think outside the box". "Draw outside the lines" and even "Think like there is NO BOX." Part your hair on the other side today. My father actually did that once and no one noticed. He was so dejected. But he knew it was different. He had been just a little bit wild and crazy that day.

Don't think
OUTSIDE
★ ★ ★ THE BOX ★ ★ ★
Think like
THERE
is no box

When you think of flexibility, think of a pole vaulters pole. When the athlete runs down the track and places that pole it is straight. He then leaps in the air and the pole begins to bend. It bends backward... and back... and it looks like it might break.

Then it starts to right itself, and the vaulter goes flying up in an amazing feat to unfathomable heights... over that bar... totally defying gravity... Wow!

We are often inflexible because we are scared. We like security. We like things to stay the same and never change. Embrace change. Change is your friend.

"The secret of change is to focus all of your energy, not on fighting the old, but on building the new."

Socrates
Classical Greek Philosopher

Develop your Curiosity

Have you ever wondered how things are made? I love those TV shows that tell us those kinds of things.

Look around your world and think about all the fascinating things that happen every day that we take for granted. We flip on the light switch and light comes on. How does that really work? We hold little gadgets up to our ear and hear someone talk to us, or better yet we see them on video chat. Seriously, "Beam me up Scotty!" We are living in fantastic times.

I challenge you to look at the world through the eyes of a child. Ask why? How? What if?

This will develop your curiosity and help you think of more and better alternatives when faced with life's roadblocks.

Take a minute to think about:

- What would you like to know more about

- Look it up

- Go to a library

- Smell the old books, *I love the smell of old books*

Step 5 was using creativity to think of alternative solutions. We can use the Super Powers of Creativity, Flexibility, and Curiosity to help us discover alternative solutions. Next we will explore Step 6 in our 7 step process.

Step 6: Make an Educated Decision

Using Decisiveness, and Good Judgment

"The more decisions that you are forced to make alone, the more you are aware of your freedom to choose."

Thornton Wilder
American playwright and novelist

Okay, so we know some stuff. We have looked at all the alternatives we can possibly find.

Here is the big moment....
Step 6 is **make a decision.**

This can be the hardest part of the Wiggle process for many people because it means making a commitment. What if you are wrong?

Well, let's think about that. What if you are wrong? Is it the end of the world? Not in the Wiggle method. Because if it doesn't work out going this way, you can try another choice. That is not to say, go back and forth like a cat watching a mouse ping pong game. You need to give the first choice a chance to pan out before you call it a bad choice. Stick with it for a while. If it is a true change, give it a month.

Build the Power of Decisiveness

Building the ability to make decisions requires practice. So, start exercising the decision muscle. When your significant other asks, "Where do you want to go for dinner?" Instead of saying, "I don't know, where do you want to go?" Make a choice. They might say, "No, I don't want to go there…" But that's a whole other problem. You just need to start making some decisions.

Your decisions don't have to all be right either. Just take your best guess. Look at your options, analyze what you know about it, and decide. If you feel strongly about the choice, you can argue about it with your significant other. If you do not, don't waste the energy. Just make another choice when they say, "No, I don't want to go there…" But do not give in to the easy method of letting someone else decide everything for you.

Sometimes we don't make decisions because we are afraid of being wrong. We may have memories of being chastised for making bad decisions in the past. The fear of being wrong can cause some people to freeze up and they simply stop making decisions. If this sounds familiar, realize that…

IT IS OK TO MAKE A MISTAKE.

This is the great part about wiggling. If you make a wrong turn, just pick another route. If you make the wrong decision, you are not stuck with it.

Life is an everchanging existence.

There are cycles that happen all around us. The ebb and flow of the ocean tide, light and sound waves have amplitude peaks and valleys. Even if it appears to be something static or solid, life is made up of tiny particles of matter that are ever changing.

So, it is NO BIG DEAL to make a wrong decision. Just start exercising your right to decide.

We all have things that cause us great stress for silly reasons. For instance, I have a spill phobia. Yep. I freak out when I spill something. After it was pointed out to me that my reaction to spills seems to be over the top, I realized that when growing up, it was a HUGE thing to my mother if I or my sister spilled something. She was so worried about the carpet or the THINGS getting messed up. Thus, I was taught that spills are a big deal. Well, they are NOT, and neither is making a wrong decision.

If it is an important decision, it is sometimes a good idea to sleep on it. That is, take a break from thinking about the problem and let your ideas ferment overnight. When you wake with a rested mind, reflect on your thoughts again and make that decision.

The Power of Wisdom

We talked about Good Judgment earlier, but it is important to revisit here. Without Good Judgment we would make flat out bad decisions, and of course no one wants to do that. We want to be WISE in our choices.

When I think about judgment, the symbol of Lady Liberty with the scales comes to mind. To me she is symbolic of Fairness, Justice, WISDOM, and Rightness. By using some of the traits we have already discussed, such as observation, analysis, and critical thinking, we are setting ourselves up to make wise and informed choices.

That is good judgment and using the power of wisdom. Weighing the known factors against each other, analyzing the evidence, and coming up with a fair solution.

One way to check your judgment is to talk to someone else about the choice. Do they see it as a fair choice? Is it wise? Does it make sense? Even by explaining your thought process to a friend, you are exercising your ability of good judgment through practice.

Next consider the comments of your friend. Analyze whether their thoughts are helpful. Take time to think about it. Then decide what you are going to do with the information. Be objective, not subjective.

Objectivity is when you look at something as if you were on the outside looking in. You consider the situation without personal attachment to the information. You are impartial.

Subjectivity is when you think about things from the inside out. That is, you are the center of the thoughts and you are not able to see the thing you are analyzing because of your personal feelings, tastes, and opinions (your biases).

The goal is to be without those biases. Try to keep your personal feelings out of the decision.

OK, so now we have made a decision. Onward to the final step...

Drum roll please!

Step 7: Take Action!

Using Bravery, Confidence, and Leadership

"Happiness is not something ready made. It comes from your own actions."

Dalai Lama
Buddhist Spiritual Leader, Monk

We made our choice, now it is time for bravery, confidence, and leadership. We have to put on the red slippers and the gold cape of the Super Hero and take a leap. DO IT!

Develop Bravery and Confidence

Bravery is facing your fears. We consider it brave for movie Super Heroes to face the villain, take a stand and fight the fight. It is the same thing in our lives. If you are faced with a trauma, disaster, or a really crappy day, the brave thing to do is take a stand and fight it.

Some days that is really hard! There are times when it is so much easier to take a bubble bath and drink a glass of wine.

In order to build the Super Power of Bravery, you have to face the things you do not want to face. You don't have to do them all at one time. Take one thing and face it.

Do you have any particular fears?

Do you have certain things you procrastinate?

Do you have something you just don't like but must do?

One thing a lot of people dislike is talking on the phone about business. Making a sales call can be one of the worst things ever. Some people have anxiety attacks over the thought of making cold calls. For those people, one way to overcome the phone phobia is practicing with a person, but back to back. By sitting back to back it is simulating the phone conversation, because you are unable to see each other. Practicing the "sales call" also allows you to put your thoughts together and feel more prepared.

Another task that makes people uncomfortable is to ask for help. Many of us like to be independent and self-sufficient, and asking for help is really difficult. Asking for help makes us feel weak in some way.

But here is the thing... we do not live on an island, well most of us that is. We all need each other to survive. Furthermore, people like to help. People like to be needed. So, if you think about it, you are helping them by asking for help.

Think about a fear you might like to face. How can you move toward overcoming that fear? More confidence might help you face the thing that is troubling you.

Recognize Your Success

Confidence is the feeling that you can rely on something or someone. Knowing that your family member will help you in a crisis. Knowing that your significant other loves you no matter what you do. They may be mad at you for a while, but they will always love you. Having those things and others like it give you confidence.

Self-Confidence comes with success. Throughout this book we have talked about taking small steps several times. The reason we want to take small steps is two-fold:

1. You want to see positive results and you don't want to make huge mistakes.

2. If you take small steps the potential for disaster is minimized. But more importantly, the potential for success is maximized.

Using the behavioral technique of successive approximation is also a nice way to build a pattern of success. Successive Approximation is a technique introduced by B.F. Skinner[9], whereby you reward for change that is close to what you are looking for, and then take steps to get closer and closer to the final result.

---

[9] Skinner, B.F., (1938) *The Behavior of Organisms*

The concept is easy to understand when thinking about dog training. Let's say we want the dog to go through an agility tunnel. If the dog is afraid of the tunnel for instance, we might start rewarding for taking a step toward the tunnel. Once that is mastered, we can then reward for looking inside the tunnel. At that point you drop the reward for walking toward it.

After the dog looks in the tunnel with ease, you might make the next step going into the tunnel partially. Agility practice tunnels are usually flexible and extendable, so you can make the tunnel short. After going in slightly, the next step might be to go through a short tunnel and the reward is given at the other side. Each step is extended toward the final goal and rewarded progressively.

You can use the same technique to reward yourself after accomplishing the small steps that eventually reach the desired goal. If you want to lose weight, you could reward yourself for healthy behaviors, such as drinking enough water during the day, exercising a small amount etc. Then the goals increase as you master the small success. This will build your confidence that you are able to do the behaviors and help you reach your goal.

Motivation

Motivation is an interesting thing. What makes you get excited about something or gives you the desire to take action? Some people are motivated by money or objects. Others get excited about the idea of taking a vacation or spending time at home with their loved ones. The key to motivating yourself or motivating others is you have to find the trigger that gets you / them going.

Triggers are the stimulus, or the carrot at the end of the fishing pole that makes the horse move the cart. What is your carrot?

To find out what motivates you think about the following:

- If you could have anything no matter how you would pay for it, what would it be?

- If you could do anything you want today, what would you do?

- When you were a child, what did you like to do?

- What makes you smile?

By thinking about your answers to these questions you can develop an understanding of what motivates you.

These are the things to focus on as you Wiggle your way through life. Keep the carrot in sight, even if you have to do something else to "take care of business."

Try to keep life fun and entertaining by giving yourself some rewards. If you have a main goal of saving $5,000 for something you want to buy, let yourself have a reward for saving certain increments ($100, $500 or $1,000 for instance).

If you want to lose 100 lbs that's a big goal. So, reward yourself when you lose the first 10 lbs, 25 lbs, 50 lbs, etc. It might not be a great idea to reward yourself with something that makes you gain back a bunch of weight. But maybe a new outfit or gadget that you've been wanting would be a good reward.

Rewards do not have to be financial either. You can give yourself time off, take a nap, watch a movie on TV, or go visit your family.

The Key is to Reward Yourself in Your Way

Another motivator is to give yourself a little pep rally. I used to work with a guy who had a "happy dance". When he solved a big problem or received a 5-star rating from a customer, he did his happy dance.

Since we all have Super Powers, I think it is only fitting that we sometimes bolster our confidence and create a little motivation by occasionally thinking of ourselves as a Super Hero! If you want to get into it, you could superimpose your face on your favorite comic Super Hero picture and look at it regularly.

Another way to feel like a Super Hero is to use your powers of creativity to come up with a whole profile of yourself as a Super Hero. Think about what you might be able to accomplish.

I would like to have Super Hero music that plays in the background as I walk around. Maybe an app on my phone with different theme songs... *Here I come to crush the day...I'm kicking butt, get out of my way...*

Thoughts on Leadership

The last step of the Wiggle method is to Take Action. The kind of Leadership we are talking about here is in reference to the actions taken. If we are using the traits of the Wiggle method, the decisions will be thought out and most likely solid decisions. By taking action on them, we are leading people and ourselves down the right path.

Things to avoid when taking action are moving too slowly, trying to be perfect, lacking confidence that you made the right choice, or hesitating. The people who you are responsible to lead will sense your lack of confidence and will start to doubt the quality of the decision. More importantly, you will doubt your decisions and start second guessing yourself. That is not productive.

Sometimes taking actions mean taking risks. Taking educated, well thought out risks are the way to move forward. Remember Edison? If it does not work out, you just found one way that doesn't work.

Warning: Do not take risks just for the thrill of it or to make yourself be bold.

Try some small steps first. Or break the major project into small parts and try the first step of the large project. But remember that nothing happens if you don't take action.

Using What You Have Learned

The Wiggle process combines many character strengths or Super Powers into a pattern of Resilience that allows you to manage almost any situation. With these traits, you are able to navigate the most winding, weed filled, rocky roads you might be facing.

It takes practice and the development of your Super Powers so that they come automatically in order to easily use these solutions when the time comes. The good thing is, you already have these traits, you just need to work on using them more often. Pick a few things you want to work on most and begin.

For your reference, here are the names of the Super Powers we have talked about in the Wiggle method:
Stay Calm
Self-Confidence
Inner Peace
Spirituality
Optimism
Listen to Your Heart
Intuition
Hope
Faith
Courage
Trust Yourself
Knowledge
Common Sense
Thinking
Good Judgment
Creativity

Flexibility
Curiosity
Decisiveness
Action
Bravery
Confidence
Leadership

The Wiggle steps are:

1. Stay Calm
2. Listen to your heart
3. Use your knowledge and common sense.
4. Evaluate the alternatives
5. Use creativity to think of any additional alternatives.
6. Make an educated decision
7. Take action!

Take a moment to think about the following situations and decide how you might apply any of the Super Powers we have discussed.

Scenario 1

Bill was a second-year student at a technical college. One day he went to school and found that the doors were locked, and his school had closed without notice.

How might you use the Super Powers to conquer this situation?

Bill's first instinct was to panic, right? He did **calm** himself down and talk to other students who were in the same boat. He used the powers of **optimism** and **hope** that the situation would resolve in a favorable manner. He sought **knowledge** about what actually happened and found out what plans were in place for the students **(common sense).** He sought **creative solutions** and was **flexible** in accepting an alternative solution that was somewhat different from his original plan. He **took action** and attended the alternative college. In fact, he was going to school to learn AC / Heating repairs and he ended up going to a different school to learn computer technologies. His path varied, but in the end, it took him to a lucrative career.

Scenario 2

I had a 17-year-old client who decided to run for student body President. On election day, the client was told by another student, who was present during the vote counts that the sister of her opponent had cheated. The sister and her friends had changed votes from the daughter to the opponent, resulting in a 2-vote difference in the favor of the opponent.

1. How would you want your daughter to deal with this situation?

2. How should the parent deal with it?

3. How do the Super Powers and the Wiggle Steps we discussed apply?

In this case, the event could be devastating to the client if winning the election was of great importance to her. Both the parent and the client are likely to be emotional and want to be reactive to the perceived afront.

If we follow the Wiggle Way, the client and mother should stay calm. Listen to their hearts. In this actual situation the daughter decided to not tell her parents. She did stay calm, and she decided that it was more important to the people who needed to cheat than it was to her. She knew in her heart and by the witness report that she actually won that election.

The possible alternatives of this situation could have been, throw a big stink and cause a lot of drama, report people, bring the witness in and make them lose face with other students. Those alternatives were not acceptable to the client. So, she decided in this case the action to take was to do nothing about it.

Scenario 3

Jeff is a 34-year-old, who has a substance abuse problem. His addiction has become a problem in all areas of his life. Subsequently, he lost his job, his wife, his home and his self-worth.

1. What would you suggest to Jeff in this case?

2. Which of the Super Powers we talked about could help Jeff?

In this case, of course Jeff needed to get some professional help with his addiction and his depression. He also began to work on Hope, Calm, and Self-Confidence. It was important that he begin to engage with other people and rebuild himself. Jeff is still in that phase and I know he will be able to create a new life for himself. It is scary and a lot of work, but I have the faith that he can do it, and when he listens to his heart, he knows he can as well.

What is Your Scenario?

1. What is going on in your life that could use a little Super Powers?

2. Which of the Super Powers above could help you?

3. What are you going to do to start developing and using that Super Power more?

Summary

Wiggling can be a fun and fulfilling exciting way to successfully navigate through life and BLAST through your problems. In order to feel comfortable with using your newly found Super Powers you have to practice using them. It is time to get a little attitude.

Start thinking about yourself as a **POWERFUL PERSON** with **SUPER** qualities. If it helps, play some super hero music. Use some affirmations to build your confidence. I have an app that allows me to make videos that are Super Hero Powers. I can Zap something, make it disappear. All of these are of course not reality, but it is fun to visualize yourself doing these Super Human type things.

Just remember, however, you are quite capable of performing **EXTRAORDINARY** feats with the Super Powers you have.

Choose a few Super Powers you would like to develop and start using them more often. Remember to take small steps at first and enjoy your successes.

I would love to hear how you use your Super Powers or how you have seen other people using them. Let me hear from you!

Email: drcobb@superpowers.life
Website: https:// superpowers.life

Remember:
You don't have to look like a super hero to BE ONE!
and
No jumping off tall buildings without a parachute!

Message from the Author

Thank you for reading this book. I hope you have found it of value to you. Please help others locate and enjoy this book in one of the following ways:

Lend: The book is lending-enabled, so feel free to share it with a friend.

Recommend: Please recommend the book to your friends, family, reading groups or social networks as applicable.

Review: If you are comfortable leaving a review on Amazon or Good Reads, please let others know why you liked the book and how you find it to be helpful.

Thanks again for your support of this book!

Appendix

The following exercises are also available in PDF from https://superpowers.life/wiggle-workbook-sign-up/

Exercise 1: Reduce Stress by Your Actions

Consider the following questions:

	Yes	No
Are you often late?		
Do you often lose things?		
Do you get 7-8 hours of sleep a night?		
Do you eat nutritious food?		
Do you consume a lot of caffeine daily?		
Do you drink 6 – 8 glasses of water a day?		
Are you argumentative?		
Do you get offended easily?		
Do you find yourself in conflicts regularly?		
Do you have a cluttered house/ car/ apartment?		
Do you rush to complete tasks?		

Think about your answers

Which of these activities might be causing you stress?

Take out some writing materials and write down one change you can make in your actions to reduce your stress:

Is that something you want to change?

If not, don't try to change it.

Look for another way you might want to change your actions to reduce stress.

Can you commit to making that change for 1 week?

If not, don't do it.

Find one thing you can commit to changing for at least 1 week. Write it down on your paper:

Exercise 2: Reduce Your Stress by Adding Something New

Consider the following ideas and pick one you can add to your life to reduce stress:

Exercise   Monitor   Meditation   Yoga   New
            Yourself   Hobby

By adding one of these activities to your life you will begin to learn to calm your body and mind. If you chose to begin one of these activities try it for at least one month. It takes practice to make any significant change.

For a review:

Exercise would be adding some form of aerobic or weight training exercise on a regular basis, such as 3 – 5 times a week for 10 – 45 minutes depending on your current level of fitness.

Monitor yourself involves using various applications to keep track of your vital signs, your blood pressure, heart rate, pulse rate, sleep, breathing, food intake, or exercise activities.

Meditation could use several types of meditation. If you chose this commit to meditating for at least 10 minutes a day 3 or more times a week.

Yoga combines exercise and meditation. There are classes or videos available to teach the basics.

If you chose to begin a **new hobby,** make sure it is something you find relaxing.

Exercise 3: Self-Confidence

Think of a time in the past when you did something well. Write it down on some paper:

What was it?

Why was it good?

What did you do really well recently?

Yesterday?

Earlier in the week?

What was good about it?

How did you feel when you did these things?

If you can't think of anything, ask someone who knows you well and is supportive. They will be able to tell you about things you do well.

Realizing what you do well helps you be more confident.

Exercise 4: Look on the Bright Side

If you are a realistic thinker, who might not see the positive side of things all the time, you might try looking at the opposite side of the situation.

1. What is something you would like to see change in your life?

2. What is your view of the situation right now?

3. What is the direct opposite view of that situation?

Most likely the true picture is somewhere between how you feel about it and the direct opposite.

Example:
  Someone might say: "I have no passion in life."

  The direct opposite of that would be "I have lots of passion or I am passionate about EVERYTHING in life."

  Reality is "There are some things I am passionate about."

Next:
  Think about the possibility that you might really be somewhere in between your current view and the opposite view. In the example – there is probably

some amount of passion each person has about something. Even if you are not able to think of what it is right now.

For the passion question:

1. Think about what do you **like** to do?

2. What did you **used to like** to do?

3. Who do you enjoy being around?

A good thing to consider is the following:

1. If I woke up tomorrow and something had changed, what would I be doing?

2. What / Who would be in my life?

3. What would the perfect situation be?

You can look at the opposite view from your current view and then try to find a happy meeting place in order to be more optimistic. I call this, *Flipping the Coin.*

Affirmations are another way to help get yourself in an optimistic frame of mind.

The next exercise is an affirmation writing task.

Exercise 5: Affirmation Writing

We go through life talking to ourselves all the time. We think thoughts about what we are doing, and what we want to do, how we feel etc. Most of these thoughts are automatic. We don't even realize when we are having such thoughts.

Affirmations are purposeful thoughts. That is one reason they may feel a little strange at first.

Affirmations can be a powerful way to get your mind in the place where you want it to be.

The way you write an affirmation is to:

1. Use words that stimulate an emotional response for you.

2. Use action words.

3. Make a statement that is personal to you.

4. The statement is in the present, even if the thing has not yet happened.

Usually they start with "I am..."

Examples:

I am happy walking on the beach next to my new condo.

Happy is the emotion. Walking on the beach is the action. Next to my new condo is visualizing the purchase of the condo that represents success and it is all in present tense.

OK – Your turn:

Write down "I am" on your page.

Then write your first affirmation.

Now write 4 more affirmations.

Now, write them on post-it notes and post them around the house where you will see them. When you see them, read it out loud to yourself. Say each one 3 times when you see it and believe the statement. See yourself as the statement describes.

The more you can do this, the more the affirmation will help you be what it states.

Some people find affirmations very helpful. Give them a try and see how you like them.

Exercise 6: Make a Pro / Con List

What is a decision you need to make?
Your Pro / Con list would look something like this...

List all the reasons why you should do solution A	List all the reasons why you should do solution B
Keep going as long as you need...	

By making an exhaustive list of all the Pros and Cons of the situation, you will usually have an idea of which is the better choice.

Exercise 7: Creativity

Think about a way you could add more creative tasks to your life:

You can actually be more creative in the way you approach almost any situation.

One way to think more creatively is to just brainstorm. Brainstorming is when you just let the thoughts about the question come out without judging them. Write down as many possible solutions to your problem as you can... good ones.... bad ones... silly ones... old or new ideas.

Write down a description of your problem:

Now write some possible solutions:

After you write all the possible solutions down, think about how you might apply those solutions.

Can they be combined with each other in a unique way?

How might you create an answer to your problem?

Creativity comes in many forms. You can do something artistic. Learn to play an instrument. Write a poem. Be creative with food.

You can go to a library or museum and appreciate works of art. Appreciation makes you more aware of creative efforts and in turn helps you be more creative.

1. Write down one way that you can start adding more creativity to your world:

2. When will you start that?

3. How often will you do it?

4. Make a commitment to yourself but be sure it is something you will and can do.

Exercise 8: Flexibility

What are you pretty rigid about?

Do you like to do certain things on a certain day of the week?

Do you have to sleep on the left side of the bed?

Do you have habits that you adhere to with precision?

If you want to try out a little more flexibility – try making a slight change in one of your more rigid areas.

1. If you would normally say, "no" to friends who want you to go do something – try saying "yes" next time.

2. If you always eat at a certain restaurant – try eating somewhere new.

3. Question yourself a little more. Why do you have to do something the way you have always done it?

Exercise 9: Motivation

Discover what motivates you:

1. What material things do you want?

2. What do you wish you had more time to do?

3. When you were a child what did you love to do?

4. What makes you smile?

5. Who would you like to spend more time with?

The things that come to mind when you think of these answers are your motivators.

By understanding what motivates you, it will be easier to find ways to kick your butt into gear when you are having a tough time getting going.

Create carrots for yourself – rewards for achieving small steps by using these things as the keys.

Exercise 10: Using Your Super Powers

The following is a list of the Super Powers discussed in this book. Write down on your paper three of these you already use on a regular basis.

Stay Calm	Self-Confidence	Inner Peace	Spirituality
Optimism	Listen to Your Heart	Intuition	Hope
Faith	Courage	Trust Yourself	Use Knowledge
Use Common Sense	Creativity	Flexibility	Curiosity
Decisiveness	Take Action	Bravery	Leadership

Now write down 3 Super Powers that you would like to continue to develop.

Do a search online and find the definition of each word.

Write down how you can start using that Super Power more today?

What is a situation that could use a little more of that Super Power right now?

Write a plan for how you are going to use those 3 Super Powers more and **GO DO IT!**

Made in the USA
San Bernardino, CA
09 October 2018